URAWAZA
SECRET EVERYDAY TIPS AND TRICKS FROM JAPAN

DO EVERYTHING BETTER!

Lisa Katayama / Illustrations by Joel Holland

CHRONICLE BOOKS

SAN FRANCISCO

Library of Congress Cataloging-in-Publication Data available.

ISBN: 978-0-8118-6215-8

Manufactured in China

Designed by Eloise Leigh and Jacob T. Gardner

10 9 8 7 6 5 4 3 2

Chronicle Books LLC
680 Second Street
San Francisco, California 94107

www.chroniclebooks.com

This book is intended as an educational and informational guide. It is important that all the instructions are followed carefully, as failure to do so could result in injury. Every effort has been made to present the information in this book in a clear, complete, and accurate manner; however, not every situation can be anticipated and there can be no substitute for common sense. The accuracy and completeness of the information provided herein and the opinions stated herein are not guaranteed or warranted to produce any particular results, and the advice and strategies contained herein may not be suitable for every individual. The authors and Chronicle Books disclaim any and all liability resulting from injuries or damage caused during the production or use of the information discussed in this book.

This book is dedicated to my two grandmas, Amy Sung and Itsu Katayama.

Amy was one of the few great female journalists in pre-Communist China. I like to think that I inherited her love of great stories and the written word.

Itsu was the original urawaza master. She once gave me a bamboo pole with a golf ball stuck to the end for knocking the stiffness out of my shoulders, and super-strong sake for my sore throat.

CONTENTS

CHAPTER THREE:
BEAUTY SCHOOL 101

HOUSEHOLD HACKS CONT'D

BEHIND THE CUPBOARD DOOR

CHAPTER SIX:
LAUNDRY SHORTCUTS

06

STREET SMARTS FOR THE GREAT OUTDOORS

INTRODUCTION

U·ra·wa·za \ 'oo rah wah zah (noun):
1. a secret trick; 2. an unmapped shortcut

I was born in a small hospital less than five minutes from
Roppongi, Tokyo's bustling nightlife district. My parents
weren't rich, but they had the means to buy what they
needed to raise two kids in a big city. The Japanese econ-
omy was booming. Growing up, my younger brother and I
had fresh salmon from the fish guy, organic beef from the
meat shop up the street, piping-hot sweet potatoes from
the sweet-potato man's truck, toy cars and Barbie dolls
from the toy shop nearby, and pretty much everything else
we needed from the general store on Roppongi Road.
Being a child of Tokyo in the 1980s was not, by any means,
a struggle for survival, and in the years following, the city's
obsession with consumer culture only grew bigger. But
today's urban landscape of neon signs, soaring skyscrapers,
and the *manga*-reading, blinged-out-cell-phone-carrying,
karaoke room–dwelling Tokyoites didn't just sprout out of
nowhere. Today's Japan is a product of the generations
before it, who literally built the country back up from the
ashes of war on not much more than a solid work ethic and
a penchant for innovation.

THE HISTORY OF URAWAZA

The concept of homespun tips and tricks in Japan predates World War II, but it was in the immediate postwar period that such innovation came in especially handy. By the design of the occupation government, directed by the United States, the new Japan was to be peace-loving, nonaggressive, and focused on economic growth. But the country was nearly starting from scratch. By the end of the war, many of Japan's major cities had been destroyed, and the country's resources had been exhausted. Basic provisions like food and cleaning supplies were hard to come by.

All over the country, in many ways, people were trying to discover how to do more with less. Fictional characters such as Astro Boy used their superpowers to inspire progress toward a bright yet challenging future. Engineers and researchers in newly formed companies like Sony and Sanyo experimented with electronics, emphasizing efficiency and miniaturization. Japanese housewives also tried to figure out how to wring the most uses out of the limited supplies available, saving money in the process.

Imagine a young woman in a suburb of Tokyo standing at her kitchen counter, pondering a single bundle of spinach. She bought it to feed the family for dinner, but she's trying to figure out what else she can do with it. She boils the spinach, and the water turns green. Can this be turned into soup broth? She tastes it. It's bitter. But why waste good water just because it's green or tastes bad? So she washes her face with it. After all, that bar of soap has been making her skin scaly and dry—maybe the spinach has nutrients that would be good for the skin. A week of doing this and her face is smoother than it had been using facial cream, a luxury expense that can now be crossed off the shopping list. She has saved the family a bunch of money and extended the usefulness of the spinach water.

Even today, Japanese families often live in relatively small quarters with little room for an overabundance of devices and supplies, even if they are able to afford them. And, unlike as in the cheap-and-quick service culture in the United States, manicures and professional dry-cleaning in Japan come at pretty hefty prices. These factors, combined with an enterprising spirit that spans generations, have yielded a treasure trove of useful tips and tricks that make everyday life just a little bit easier.

In the consumer culture of today, it's easy to *not* have to think up innovative uses for ordinary things. Aisles and aisles of cleaning supplies and convenience items have rendered creative economizing almost completely unnecessary. If you want to clean the kitchen tile, or the bathtub, or the windows, you can simply buy specialized products for each of those purposes. But urawaza have appeal beyond strict necessity. Nonchemical solutions to cleaning messes or stains, for example, avoid environmental and health consequences, and sometimes a simple home remedy is simply more effective than using a store-bought product for a common ailment. Plus, there's something oddly satisfying and fun about being resourceful and discovering new adaptabilities to everyday challenges. There's a certain "Wow!" factor to knowing that you have an organic, quirky cure for just about any ailment or household accident, that you can walk around in high heels in pouring rain without slipping, or that you know how to make your sled the fastest on the slope on a snowy day. Urawaza can save you money, earn you style points, impress your family, and amaze your friends.

DISCOVERING URAWAZA

When I was in third grade, I thought it would be funny to write "I HATE MS. NICHOL!" all over my homeroom teacher's whiteboard. But Ms. Nichol didn't think so, especially when she discovered that I had mistakenly used a permanent pen instead of a whiteboard marker. As a punishment, I was forced to stay after class and figure out how to erase the board while everyone else was outside playing Capture the Flag. I tried rubbing the words with chalk, dry fingers, greasy fingers, a wet whiteboard eraser, a plastic umbrella, soap from the girls' bathroom, and even my homework notebook, but nothing worked. Desperate and scanning the classroom's contents once again, I saw a rubber eraser sitting at the corner of the in-house math genius's desk. I picked it up and rubbed it against the word *HATE* written in barely legible cursive letters across the center of the board. To my great delight, the *H* began to disappear, leaving a glossy patch of white where the defamatory declaration used to be. "Look, Ms. Nichol!" I exclaimed. "It comes off with an eraser!" Ms. Nichol still looked pissed, but I was exhilarated. I was free to play Capture the Flag, and I had just discovered my first urawaza.

It's been almost twenty years since that fateful day, and these surprise discoveries are still coming my way in different shapes and forms. When I brought my dog, Ruby, back to Tokyo one summer a few years ago, she and my parents' dogs went on a four-month-long peeing spree throughout the house. It was a constant battle for territory. First, Ruby would mark her turf, then Birdie would follow, then Ryukun would spray the entire wall. I would scream at all three of them, then run downstairs to the supply cabinet and grab the carpet cleaner. Shake, spray, let sit for two minutes, and scrub away with the attached brush. It was easy, and required only that one bottle, but I began to notice after several days of repeating this procedure that the patches of carpet I doused with foam were turning whiter than the rest of the cream-colored carpet fabric. Uh-oh. And then I saw my mother's solution to the routine canine pee fest—pat the mess with a dry pad, then dampen the spot with water and absorb it with a second pad, then apply a tiny bit of dish soap and pat dry yet again. This removed the spots and smells perfectly without bleaching the carpet or using anything more exotic or chemical than the soap.

Thankfully, the dogs don't pee on the carpet anymore, but if they ever do, I now know an urawaza solution that is much more organic, inexpensive, and effective than the store-bought one. When I asked my mom where she learned how to do this, she said, "I just figured out that this was the best way after forty years of dog ownership."

The term *urawaza* was coined by the video-game industry in the early 1980s, when gamers found secret in-game commands that allowed them to power up or become invincible. When Nintendo released the original Super Mario Bros. in 1985, players quickly discovered that if they climbed the hidden beanstalk in world 4-2, they could warp to worlds 6, 7, and 8. There was also a place where players could step on a turtle, make its shell bounce back and forth between two green pipes, and rack up points until they were rewarded with unlimited extra lives. These tricks were actually glitches left over from when programmers creating the software needed to be able to use these shortcuts for experimentation, but they became known among gamers as "urawaza." Over the years, the term expanded beyond Nintendo's fantasy world to encompass homegrown Japanese wisdoms for everyday life. Today, these lifestyle urawaza have taken on a following of their own.

The mainstreaming of lifestyle urawaza was triggered by the advent of the weekly television show *Ito-ke no Shokutaku (The Ito Family Dinner Table)* in 1997. Each episode of *Ito-ke*, hosted by Japanese celebrities posing as a family, featured an entertaining lineup of viewer-generated ideas on how to use daily objects in the most unlikely ways. At its peak, it had an impressive viewership of nearly 30 percent of Japanese households. In the last few years, the sharing of these household tips and tricks has proliferated to generate Web sites, online bulletins, and numerous books showcasing the phenomenon. Mixi, a social-networking site, has several urawaza communities that include more than 25,000 active participants who share advice and topics divided into categories such as kitchen, technology, and dating.

So, don't be surprised if your Japanese friend uses an orange to give herself the perfect manicure, or whips out a wine bottle in the karaoke bar to help hit those high notes in her favorite Mariah Carey tunes. Urawaza are part of a secret body of knowledge inherent in our culture that yields inventive new ways of looking at objects in relation to everyday dilemmas. With this book, you can stop gaping at the distance runner tying a rubber band around his toe, and participate in the quirky, utilitarian fun.

CHAPTER ONE:
HEALTHY HINTS FOR SICK DAYS

Every family has its own version of what to do
when the kids catch a cold, and these methods—
whether scientifically proven or not—are passed
down from generation to generation, providing
the sick with a sense of safety and comfort.
My Japanese grandma always had a remedy for
everything—it was so much fun being ill in her
presence that I actually *wanted* (and sometimes
pretended) to be sick every time I visited her
home in Kyushu. Here are some urawaza to try
on those not-so-made-up sick days.

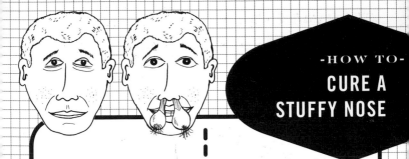

DILEMMA:

Your nose feels like it's stuffed with cotton, and your sinuses are about to explode. Over-the-counter medicines aren't helping, and you're desperate for a quick, easy fix to your persistent breathing difficulties.

SOLUTION:

Scallions are good for more than just dressing up a bowl of ramen. Simply cut the top fronds off two green onions, stick the remaining thick white root sections into your nostrils, and let your new nose plugs do their thing. Your sinuses will magically clear up—plus, you don't have to deal with drippy boogers.

WHY THIS WORKS:

Scallions are part of the onion family. Members of this plant group have irritating compounds, like burn-free sulfur-containing amino acids, that cause the hotness and sting that makes our eyes tear, our nose runny, and our mouth hot when we eat or even handle them. Putting these irritating compounds right up there by your sinuses will start the juices flowing, alleviating nasal stuffiness.

-HOW TO-
CURE A SORE THROAT

DILEMMA:

You have a sore throat and a trachea full of phlegm, but you really don't feel like dolling up to go buy cough syrup at the supermarket. All you have in your pantry is an old towel and a liter of distilled spirit wine.

SOLUTION:

Sprinkle a face towel with some *shochu* (a popular Japanese distilled liquor) and place the soaked section around your neck.

WHY THIS WORKS:

Living skin cells are sensitive to high levels of alcohol, and because *shochu* is a strong liquor, it irritates your skin's surface. Irritation causes an increase in blood flow, which can expedite healing and alleviate throat pain. The vapors from the alcohol can also help relieve a stuffy nose. But don't expect anyone to believe you when you try to explain the suddenly half-empty bottle of booze.

DILEMMA:

First, the kids were sick. Now you're feeling hot and sweaty, and your body temperature's clocking in at over 100 degrees.

SOLUTION:

Warm your feet in a bucket of hot water, then put on a pair of cold, wet cotton socks and cover that pair with a dry woolen pair. This will bring your body temperature down a few notches.

WHY THIS WORKS:

This technique, sometimes called hydrotherapy, urges the blood and lymphatic fluids to circulate to your feet to fight off the wetness. This movement stimulates the immune system, putting the body in a parasympathetic state and triggering the healing process.

EASE UP STIFF SHOULDERS

DILEMMA:

You've been sitting in front of your laptop all day, every day, for about five years now, and your shoulders feel like two enormous rocks. Rocks with piercing pain. But who has time to go get a professional massage?

SOLUTION:

Stick two pieces of adhesive tape on your face—from the outer corner of each eye to your temples—so they're pulling lightly at the area near your eyes.

WHY THIS WORKS:

Often, sore shoulders are linked to tension in your entire upper body, including your facial muscles. By taping the skin near your temples, you're stretching out your forehead muscles, alleviating tension and letting them feel more relaxed.

DILEMMA:

You just got off the airplane, where you were sandwiched between a noisy baby and a man with horrible sleeping habits. Dodging flailing arms and legs and keeping your ears plugged for thirteen hours has rendered your spine completely achy and stiff.

SOLUTION:

The secret to curing a backache lies in a popular condiment—mustard. Simply combine one part mustard powder with two parts flour and stir the mixture into water until you make a nice paste, then spread it onto a warm towel and drape the towel, mustard-side out, across your back.

WHY THIS WORKS:

Mustard causes minor irritations on the skin, increasing blood circulation and causing a warm tingling that alleviates pain. This remedy, called a mustard plaster, was part of early American medicine, too.

WARNING: Check your back every few minutes to avoid overexposure, and do not let the mustard come into direct contact with your skin—it is an irritant.

STAY WARM AFTER A BATH

DILEMMA:

You love how your body feels hot and heavy from quality time alone in the bathtub, but cooling off afterward is such a buzz kill. Isn't there a way to prolong the warm fuzzies?

SOLUTION:

Suck on an ice cube minutes before you come out of the bath to significantly prolong the sensation of warmth.

WHY THIS WORKS:

Your body cools down quickly after you emerge from a bath because the water evaporates from your skin and cool air lowers your body temperature. Sucking on an ice cube is sort of like eating ice cream— it makes you feel cool inside and decreases the contrast with your surroundings, so when you get out of the tub the air doesn't seem so frigid.

DILEMMA:

You love to go hiking in the snowy mountains during wintertime, but your petite frame gets cold easily, and you're always shivering. You need a quick remedy for the chills that doesn't require you to carry a backpack full of extra layers.

SOLUTION:

The Japanese custom of bowing isn't just useful for showing respect. It also helps you stay warm. Give the imaginary honorable person before you ten deep bows and you'll feel warm all over, physically and in spirit.

WHY THIS WORKS:

Though almost any kind of movement when you're cold will help warm your body, the deep bowing gesture is particularly effective in stimulating your arteries and nerves to increase blood circulation. There's a thick artery that runs right through your solar plexus area, the part that contracts and relaxes when you bow.

PREVENT FROSTBITTEN TOES

DILEMMA:
You have really bad circulation in your limbs, and every time you take your dog out for a walk on a cold winter day, your toes freeze up and turn purple.

SOLUTION:
Put a chile pepper inside your sock at the tip of your shoe to save your poor little piggies from frostbite.

WHY THIS WORKS:

Chile peppers contain a chemical called capsaicin, which is secreted by the placenta surface cells on the inside lining of the fruit. Capsaicin has the effect of making your body feel warmer, which is why eating hot foods can make you sweat. Putting one in your shoe isn't as effective as eating one, but some capsaicin from inside the pepper reaches its outer surface, and warmth can be transmitted through physical contact.

DILEMMA:

There's nothing worse than musty feet with fungus between the toes. Yuck. But that's what happens when you keep your feet holed up in your superthick socks and heavy-duty sneakers on a hot, sweaty day of playing football.

SOLUTION:

When you get home from a humid day, put some hot water in a giant bowl or pan. Crush a clove or two of garlic, put it in the hot water, and soak your feet in it for ten minutes.

WHY THIS WORKS:

This footbath not only feels great, it also prevents nasty fungus growth. Garlic has more than a hundred chemically active compounds that do wonderful things such as prevent cancer, lower blood pressure, and kill the fungus that leads to athlete's foot.

PREVENT BODY ODOR

DILEMMA:

Soap keeps you feeling fresh for a few minutes out of the shower, and deodorant masks the smell for a few hours thereafter, but by the end of the day, your armpits smell like a funky mix of sweat, dust, and fake baby powder.

SOLUTION:

A natural deodorant made of baking soda and lemon juice works better than almost any over-the-counter stick. Just dust some baking soda on your pits, rub some lemon juice on top, and pat dry for natural, stink-free crevices.

WHY THIS WORKS:

Baking soda absorbs moisture and kills odor-causing bacteria, and the acidity of the lemon changes the pH balance of your skin. Because bacteria don't do so hot in high acidity, they tend not to proliferate in a lemony environment.

-HOW TO-
GET RID OF SURFACE SPLINTERS

DILEMMA:

You have dozens of little splinters in your hands and arms from helping your little brother with his secret wooden fort. Isn't there a way to get rid of them without having to pluck each and every one out with tweezers?

SOLUTION:

Dip your finger in a tub of liquid glue and smear it all over the problem area. Once it dries, peel it off, just the way you used to when you were a bored little kid in arts-and-crafts class. The splinters will come right out along with the peeling glue!

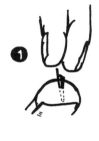

WHY THIS WORKS:

Surface splinters are hard to get out not because they're deeply embedded but because they're tiny and hard to grasp with even the daintiest of fingers. The sticky glue serves a function similar to a lint roller when the glue is applied evenly across the splintery surface of your skin. Plus, it's superfun to peel glue off your hands.

KEEP WOUNDS FROM REOPENING

DILEMMA:

That nasty cut on your elbow just won't stay closed. Every time you bend your arm to do push-ups or to scratch your back, the wound opens up again. How is it ever going to heal?

SOLUTION:

Once your blood clots, bind your easy-to-reopen boo-boo with superglue for a clean heal.

WHY THIS WORKS:

The superglue keeps the wound sealed and prevents it from popping open again. It comes off in a couple days from natural wear and tear, but by then the cut will have scabbed a little and won't reopen again. The active ingredient in superglue is cyanoacrylate, the same scab-inducing component found in liquid bandages.

DILEMMA:

Sleeping over at your boyfriend's house is like setting up camp next to a temperamental donkey. Every few minutes, his roaring snore knocks you out of your peaceful dreams, rendering you tired and cranky by the time morning rolls around.

SOLUTION:

At bedtime, tape an orange, a tennis ball, or some other spherical object between his shoulder blades. He will be uncomfortable if he turns to sleep on his back, and it's not invasive like a face mask designed to curb snoring—or a slap in the chest.

WHY THIS WORKS:

When you sleep flat on your back, the flesh of your throat relaxes, blocking airways to the nose and throat and inducing the dreaded snore. When a noisy sleeper has no choice but to sleep on his side, you (and he) are more likely to get an uninterrupted, good night's rest.

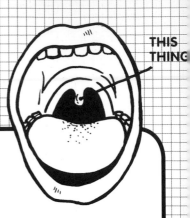

THIS THING

-HOW TO-
STOP THE HICCUPS

DILEMMA:

You've tried everything—drinking water while bending over, swallowing sugar, even reciting an old Salvadoran chant—but nothing seems to work. Now you have to pee from all the water, and you're on the world's biggest sugar high, but your life is still being interrupted every few seconds with annoying minijumps.

SOLUTION:

Open your mouth wide and touch one end of a cotton swab or the eraser end of a pencil to the back of your throat. For a second, you'll feel like gagging, and then your hiccups will stop.

WHY THIS WORKS:

When you poke at the back of your throat, you stimulate the uvula, the little piece of flesh hanging in the back of your oral cavity. That triggers a gag reflex, which interrupts the spasms coming from your diaphragm and lets you breathe in peace.

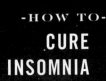

DILEMMA:

There's a lot on your mind, and you're having trouble falling asleep. You tried counting sheep, and you even brought your old high school math textbook to bed with you, but nothing's making you drowsy.

SOLUTION:

Eat some oatmeal before you hit the sack.

WHY THIS WORKS:

Oats contain an amino acid called tryptophan, which increases the amount of serotonin, a relaxation-inducing chemical, in the brain. Adding milk to the oatmeal provides a dose of carbohydrates, which helps the tryptophan get to the brain and thus helps with the serotonin production. Tryptophan is also found in bananas, yogurt, and turkey.

CURE AILMENTS WITH THE PUSH OF A FINGER

DILEMMA:

Maybe it's age. Maybe it's bad posture. Maybe it was all those push-ups you did at the gym yesterday after a six-month hiatus from exercise. Whatever the reason, your shoulders are sore, your neck is stiff, your lower back feels like it's being pinched with a giant pair of tweezers, your legs are cramping, and you're getting dizzy and constipated.

SOLUTION:

Press on the correct *tsubo*, or pressure point, for each ache or pain you're experiencing and you'll feel nice and refreshed the next day.

WHY THIS WORKS:

Though pressure points can often be very far away from the problem area, they have been discovered, after centuries of experimentation, to be effective in alleviating pain. The nerves and blood vessels in our body connect obscure points in our hands and feet to the roots of all kinds of ailments. Here are some you can try at home right now.

DIZZINESS: There is a tsubo between your right thumb and index finger. Press down about three-quarters of an inch in from the gap between the two fingers.

CHILLS: On your back, locate the midpoint between your tailbone and your waist and push the two pressure points half an inch to the right and left of it.

CONSTIPATION: Follow the end of your right pinkie finger to your outer wrist and push the indent to the immediate below left of the little bone on the corner. You'll be pooping again in no time!

BACK PAIN: There are two tsubos on the back of your left hand. The first is midway down the hand (not counting the fingers) to the right of the bone leading to the index finger. The second is to the immediate left of the bone leading to the ring finger.

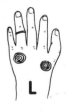

STIFF SHOULDERS: On either of your arms, mentally divide the segment between your wrist and your elbow in thirds and push the pressure point one-third of the way down from the elbow.

CHAPTER TWO:
AMAZE YOUR FRIENDS

There are many ways to be the best in something in Japan, even though they're not always as practical or honorable as you'd want them to be. On numerous highly entertaining variety television shows, contestants vie to be number one—the person who can collect the most sweat in a test tube, the person who can gain the most weight from eating unlimited amounts of sushi in an hour, or the person who can stay in a freezing-cold bath the longest. You don't have to be athletic, good looking, or even remotely talented in the conventional sense to be somebody in Japan. Here are several obscure, random ways you can one-up your friends with just a little bit of practice.

DILEMMA:

You just got a brand-new red sled for speeding down the bunny slopes, but the snow is slushy, and there's too much traction for a speedy slide.

SOLUTION:

Cover the bottom of the sled with nonstick cooking spray and get ready to whiz down the mountain like a bolt of lightning.

WHY THIS WORKS:

Nonstick cooking spray works on sleds the way ski wax works on skis. It's greasy, and greasy means slippery, and slippery means greater velocity on the downhill. Wheeee!

HIT HIGH NOTES IN KARAOKE

DILEMMA:

You want to rock those Celine Dion hits at the company karaoke fest next week, but you just can't reach the high notes at the climax of that *Titanic* song.

SOLUTION:

Just hold a full wine bottle up to your chest while you sing, and watch your spectators' jaws drop open as you score 100 on the karaoke machine.

WHY THIS WORKS:

Lifting heavy weights makes your muscles tense up, and, as a result, your vocal cords—also a muscle—stretch. This stretch allows the larynx to vibrate faster, and you'll be belting those high-pitched tunes with ease.

WARNING: Doing this continuously could strain your vocal cords, so save it for special occasions.

DILEMMA:

Moving to a new place can be fun, but hauling all those heavy boxes full of books, clothes, and random paraphernalia from old apartment to moving truck and from moving truck to new apartment is a huge pain.

SOLUTION:

Place a heavy box on top of an empty one the same or larger size and hold the bottom one to carry them. The full box will feel more like a cuddly, compact miniature pinscher than a giant pit bull.

WHY THIS WORKS:

How heavy a load feels largely depends on the center of gravity. An object will feel significantly lighter when carried at a higher position.

-HOW TO-
MAKE A BABY STOP CRYING

DILEMMA:

Sure, the baby's cute. But why won't he stop crying?

SOLUTION:

The secret to stop a crying baby lies in making the sound you produce during the mouthfeel stage of wine tasting.

WHY THIS WORKS:

When babies are still in the womb, the noises they can hear are limited to those in the 6000–8000mHz range. The sound you make when you slosh the liquid behind your lips during wine tasting takes place at about 7000mHz, reminding the baby of a time when the world around was peaceful and the whirs and stirs inside Mommy's tummy soothed him back to a sleepy state.

44

DILEMMA:

You're at the beach for your kid's birthday, and she and her friends have a gazillion little beach balls and donut floats waiting to be blown up. You have to think of a way to do this—quickly, before they get bored—without passing out from lack of oxygen.

SOLUTION:

Hold a medium-sized garbage bag open and wave it around to fill it with air. Stick one end of a drinking straw into the tube tip of the donut float, and wrap the opening of the inflated garbage bag around the other end, then slowly deflate the garbage bag.

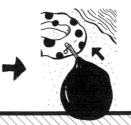

WHY THIS WORKS:

When you wave the garbage bag around, you're filling it with air. The straw serves as the transferring agent of this air supply to the kiddy floats. By collecting air with the garbage bag—which has a large, flexible opening—you save yourself the trouble of blowing your life out into the tiny tube of the donut floats.

45

KEEP A PICNIC MAT FROM FLYING AWAY

DILEMMA:

You've got the perfect date all planned out: a picnic on the beach with a bottle of wine, a foot-long baguette, a basket of brie, giant purple seedless grapes, and crunchy apples. You even brought a fancy picnic mat, but there's just one problem—its ends keep flipping up with the wind, slapping your date in the face.

SOLUTION:

There's a foolproof way to keep picnic mats from flying away that requires only four rubber bands. Tie a rubber band around each corner of the mat about one inch from the corner, then tuck the tied corners under. Your mat will be so stable, you'll think you glued it to the sand.

WHY THIS WORKS:

A picnic mat flies away when air gets underneath it, lifting it off the ground and letting it glide over the sand. When you secure the corners, you prevent air from being able to waft underneath, and the mat stays intact.

DILEMMA:

The company bowling tournament is coming up, and the winner gets an extra grand in his or her bonus this year. You want it—bad—but right now you can barely keep the ball out of the gutter.

SOLUTION:

Take an iron—yep, the one you use to press your shirts—to the bowling alley with you next time, and practice pointing the end of it at the second arrow on the right as you make your approach.

WHY THIS WORKS:

This angle positions you perfectly for a dead-center throw. When you repeat this motion without the ball first, you get the angle down pat before you factor in the weight and awkwardness of the bowling ball.

-HOW TO-
REVIVE A DYING BALLPOINT PEN

DILEMMA:

You've been pulled over for a broken taillight, and the cop's pen appears to be out of ink. You need to impress him fast before he realizes that now your left blinker's not working.

SOLUTION:

Tape a rubber band to the side of the pen, loop it over the tip, pull on both ends of the rubber band, and wind it up. Release the pen and it will twirl at a miraculous speed and redistribute the ink.

WHY THIS WORKS:

Nine times out of ten, a pen "runs out" of ink simply because air has gotten between the tip and the inkwell. To eliminate this gap, you need to use centrifugal force, the accelerating force created when an object rotates.

WARNING: Make sure you have the cap on tight while you're swinging the pen in the air! The ink could come blurting out fast and get all over your clothes—or Officer Friendly's uniform.

48

DILEMMA:

Your new girlfriend is an expert runner, but the fastest you've ever run was the time you were being chased by a flock of pigeons. She's invited you to go for a jog—and you're afraid she'll totally outshine you.

SOLUTION:

Put a rubber band around your ankle. Then stretch one end of it toward your toes and hook it over the big toe, twisting it once to make a figure eight. Repeat on your other foot.

WHY THIS WORKS:

The rubber bands help your feet expand and contract even farther than they normally do in the forefoot, where the toes connect to the foot. This provides greater power during the push-off phase of the gait cycle, enabling you to run a little faster.

FIX A SCRATCHED CD

DILEMMA:
Your friend's having a housewarming party, and he's showing off his music collection. "You should hear this one," he says, pulling an unlabeled disc from the shelf. "It's my favorite." But when he puts the disc into the CD player, it skips beats like a sample from a bad DJ performance.

SOLUTION:
Put a small amount of toothpaste on a cotton ball and gently rub it from the middle outward on the surface of the scratch. Rinse off any excess toothpaste with water and put the CD back in the player.

WHY THIS WORKS:

CDs are made of polycarbonate plastic. Small scratches on the surface of the CD can defract the laser beam that reads the data without necessarily affecting the information. Toothpaste, which acts as a mild abrasive, evens out the plastic surface and makes it play smoothly again.

DILEMMA:

It's a Friday night after a long week at work, and you just want to kick back, unwind, and get trashed. Problem is, your friends want to go to some posh bar downtown, and you have only a twenty on you. How in the world are you going to get drunk on twenty bucks at a bar that sells ten-dollar martinis?

SOLUTION:

Buy an energy drink at a liquor store and use it as a mixer.

WHY THIS WORKS:

Energy drinks have an amino acid called taurine in them, which helps speed up your metabolism. This causes you to feel the effects of the alcohol faster than you would under normal circumstances.

-HOW TO-
SWIM BACKWARD

DILEMMA:

Your breaststroke is weak, your dives all end up as belly flops, and you can't even do half a somersault without getting water up your nose. You need some kind of skill that will set you apart from the rest at the pool party this summer—but what?

SOLUTION:

Learn how to swim backward! When you flex your feet instead of pointing them while holding onto a kick-board, your body will chug through the water in reverse gear.

WHY THIS WORKS:

The direction you advance in the water depends on which way you're kicking. When you kick away from your body—which is essentially what you appear to be doing when you flex your feet—you reverse the body's inclination to go forward. It takes a little bit of practice, but once you perfect it, the whole party will be wide-eyed with wonder at your newfound skill.

52

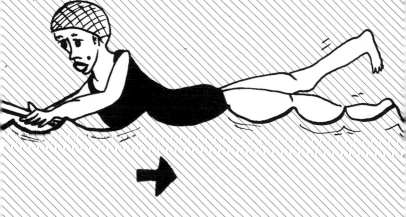

CHAPTER THREE:
BEAUTY SCHOOL 101

Reliance on organic products for beauty exists in every culture. In Japan, some of the most popular commercial skin-care products contain ingredients such as seaweed, charcoal, and the water used to wash rice. Whether you're in need of a quick fix for unexpected breakouts, an impromptu manicure on the go, or magical ways to prolong the life span of your toothbrush or a bar of soap, this chapter's got something for you.

MAKE YOUR NAILS SHINY

DILEMMA:
You do all your dishes by hand, and now your nails look dull and feel like sandpaper.

SOLUTION:
Rub a sales receipt against the surface of your nails to buff them to a waxy shine.

WHY THIS WORKS:

Sales receipts are traditionally made of thermal recording paper, the shiny "onion-skin" paper often used at gas pumps and for credit-card transactions. The tiny invisible bumps on the surface (which turn into black text when heat is applied) can serve the same purpose as a nail buffer you'd find at the drugstore. A quick scrub will make your fingernails look like you just got a manicure.

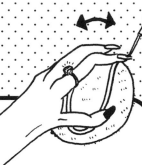

GIVE YOURSELF A PERFECT MANICURE ON THE GO

DILEMMA:

You're late for a very important date, but you didn't have time for one thing—nail polish. You even bought a new bottle to match your pretty red dress, but you're bound to screw up painting your nails on a moving train.

SOLUTION:

Grab an old tennis ball from your gym bag and hold it in your hand, nails facing toward you. Take the polish brush and sweep it across your nails for a smudge-free manicure on the go, even during your train ride.

WHY THIS WORKS:

Holding a tennis ball stabilizes your fingers, preventing them from moving and shaking. If you don't have a tennis ball, try a baseball or even a round fruit, like an apple or an orange.

DILEMMA:

After a wild night of club hopping, you're tired and hungover and have some guy's unwanted phone number scrawled on the back of your hand.

SOLUTION:

Brew yourself a cup of tea. Lightly rub the used tea bag on the part of your hand with the pen marks and watch them disappear effortlessly. You should probably drink the tea, too, to help you with the hangover.

WHY THIS WORKS:

The catechin in the tea bag mixes in with the pigments and oil content in the pen marks, making the ink float up from the skin. Tea bags are also made of nonwoven fabric, which helps scrub the ink out of the wrinkles in your hands.

SMOOTH OUT ROUGH ELBOW AND KNEE SKIN

DILEMMA:

It's winter, and the skin on your elbows and knees is so damn dry, it constantly looks a few shades whiter—and much flakier—than the rest of your body.

SOLUTION:

Avocados are delicious in salads, but they're also excellent skin-smoothing agents. Just cut the avocado in half, scoop out the insides, and rub the inside of the rind against your rough spots for a few minutes. Repeat as often as desired for maximum effect.

WHY THIS WORKS:

The oils derived from the fruit of the avocado have sterolins, or plant steroids, which help soften skin and reduce imperfections such as sun damage, age spots, and scars. These oils are similar in structure to the natural oils our skin produces. Avocados are also high in lipids—antioxidants, phospholipids, vitamins, and fatty acids—which are more easily absorbed in deep-tissue areas like the skin on our elbows or areas of extreme dryness from eczema than most other natural moisturizers.

DILEMMA:

Just when you think you're too old to be getting zits, a fresh one pops up in the middle of your forehead. Those over-the-counter acne creams make your skin dry and itchy—plus they're expensive. Isn't there a more organic way to make it go away?

SOLUTION:

Grab that bottle of apple-cider vinegar from the back of your spice cabinet and dab a tiny amount on a piece of cotton, then wipe your zit with it—believe it or not, this works as an emergency zit kit.

WHY THIS WORKS:

Vinegar contains acetic acid, which works like a light acid peel by removing dead skin and disinfecting your pores. A little dab can clean out your pores and facilitate the removal of that awful dot on your face.

WARNING: Don't try this if you have sensitive skin—the vinegar could also serve as an irritant.

GIVE YOURSELF A STEAM FACIAL IN THE TUB

DILEMMA:

They say steam is great for opening up pores and keeping skin zit-free, but there has to be a better way to do this than installing a steam sauna in your shower.

SOLUTION:

Sit in your tub with an umbrella open over your head.

WHY THIS WORKS:

The umbrella will trap the moisture under its curve and make you sweat like you just ran a mile—or spent fifteen minutes in a steam sauna.

DILEMMA:

You love your evening bath, but it always ends up cooling down a couple notches by the time your nerves calm down and your muscles start to loosen up. Your hot-water heater's usually empty by the time you've filled up the tub once, so it's not like you can keep adding hot water.

SOLUTION:

Take several chunks of orange peel and let them dry in the sun for a day. Then wrap them in a cloth bag, and let this bag float in the tub with you.

WHY THIS WORKS:

The citrus oils in orange peels increase blood circulation, making you feel warmer for longer. The oils may also form a thin protective layer on the surface of the water, reducing heat loss from the actual tub water.

TAKE AN ALL-NATURAL HOT SPRING—LIKE BATH

DILEMMA:

A hot bath is a great way to relax sore muscles, calm the mind, and wind down at the end of a long day. Unfortunately, the nearest spa is far away and expensive, and your kid won't let you borrow his strawberry bubble bath anymore.

SOLUTION:

Iris leaves, peach leaves, ginger, radish leaves, *yuzu* (an Asian citrus fruit), sake, and Epsom salt are all excellent accompaniments for a therapeutic bath.

WHY THIS WORKS:

Legend has it that iris leaves relieve sore shoulders and nerves, peach leaves are good for heat rash, ground ginger is good for blood circulation, dried radish leaves keep the body warm, yuzu is an aromatic, and sake is an exfoliate. Epsom salt has magnesium that is absorbed through the skin to reduce inflammation and relieve pain.

-HOW TO-
MAKE YOUR DULL HAIR GLOSSY

DILEMMA:
You thought it would look cool to have permed, colored, blow-dried hair, but instead your tresses are so damaged that you look like you're wearing a mop on your head.

SOLUTION:
A homemade vinegar rinse won't solve all your problems, but it will give your dull hair a little shine. Mix one part vinegar with eight parts water and apply this vinegar rinse to your scalp and mane after a shampoo. You can even leave it in to prevent tangles.

BORING!

GLOSSY!

WHY THIS WORKS:

The secret to shiny hair lies in the cuticles. Cuticles are like roof shingles—they can make your hair ragged and scaly if they're open, but they'll look shiny if they're tightly closed. Vinegar removes buildup and residue from your hair and closes the cuticles. Once closed, the hair is also much more slippery and less tangle-prone.

-HOW TO-
FIX BROKEN LIPSTICK

DILEMMA:

You take your lipstick everywhere—but the last time you went out, you forgot to put the cap back on. Never mind the bright red stains all over the inside of your bag; you're more concerned with putting your broken little stick of joy back together again.

SOLUTION:

Use a hair dryer to heat up the intact base of the lipstick for twenty seconds or so. When it's partially melted, stick the broken half on top of it, letting the two pieces meld together. Smooth out the sides so there are no jagged edges and stick it in the freezer for half an hour to let it set in place.

WHY THIS WORKS:

Lipstick contains waxes, oils, emollients, and pigments, all of which work together to create that soft, smooth, easily applicable texture. When heat is applied to it, it becomes highly pliable, and you can basically shape it however you want.

64

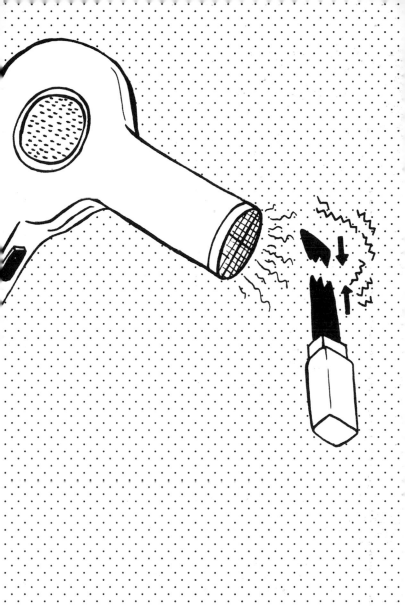

CHAPTER FOUR:
HOUSEHOLD HACKS

There's an old belief in Japan that cleaning
your toilet daily will bring you good luck. A
former rock star once testified that stock
he owned suddenly increased in value when he
started wiping his bowl daily, and during his
Golden Lion Award acceptance speech at
the Venice Film Festival in 1997, filmmaker
Takeshi Kitano reportedly claimed that he had
followed a fortune-teller's advice to do the
same. Whether it's wiping every corner of the
potty, dusting your furniture, reviving a dying
plant, or getting rid of unwanted rodent visi-
tors, there's an urawaza out there to fit your
every sanitizing need.

DUST YOUR APARTMENT

DILEMMA:

You know there are mounds of dust accumulating behind your stove and above your curtain railings because you've been sneezing nonstop. But you can't see it, and you can't figure out how to clean it without making the dust scatter throughout the room.

SOLUTION:

Elongate a wire hanger so that the hook serves as a handle and the two wings are stretched out parallel to each other, and then pull an old stocking tightly over it. Congratulations! You've just created a homemade dustbuster.

WHY THIS WORKS:

Stockings generate tons of static, so the dust sticks to it instead of spreading apart. Plus, the shape makes it supereasy to reach nooks and crannies that can't be accessed with conventional store-bought dusters.

GET LINT OFF YOUR CARPET

DILEMMA:

Dog fur, human hair, laundry lint—your carpet's full of funky, nasty stuff that you really don't want to be rolling around on. The vacuum cleaner's broken, so you need to think of another way to take care of the mess.

SOLUTION:

Strategically slide six to eight rubber bands, evenly spaced, along the surface of the cardboard core from a roll of paper towels or plastic wrap and roll your new contraption up and down your carpet in rows.

WHY THIS WORKS:

All that nastiness will get caught up in the gaps between the rubber-band rings, ridding your carpet of these unwanted bits and pieces once and for all. The stickiness of the elastic, plus the static, keeps the junk from falling out.

DILEMMA:

You just broke up with your boyfriend. You've returned all his belongings and deleted all photos of him from your computer, but a gazillion sticker pictures you took together line your bathroom mirror and refuse to come off.

SOLUTION:

Squirt some mayonnaise onto a paper towel or a tissue, rub it on the sticky surface, and wipe the stubborn adhesive off with a knife or a piece of tissue.

WHY THIS WORKS:

Mayonnaise is made of vegetable oil and egg yolk (plus all the spices that make it yummy), and it's the oil that goes to work and dissolves the adhesive. The consistency of mayonnaise makes it optimal for spreading onto almost any surface.

PICK UP BROKEN GLASS

DILEMMA:

There's no use crying over spilled milk, but a broken glass—that's something else. Isn't there a way to get rid of all the tiny shards on the floor without cutting up your hands and feet?

SOLUTION:

Lightly press a few slices of regular bread over the danger zones.

WHY THIS WORKS:

Even the tiniest fragments of glass will wedge between the holes in the bread, leaving your floor shard-free.

DILEMMA:

Every time your kid brother has his friends over to watch a game and eat pizza, they leave their greasy fingerprints all over the living room, depositing enough grub for the roaches to have an after-party on.

SOLUTION:

To prevent the roaches from getting past cracks in the walls, place some of that leftover soda from your brother's party in shallow bowls near the cracks and other entry points around the room. When your brother wakes up in the morning, he'll find his roach buddies floating in brown syrup.

WHY THIS WORKS:

Soda is sweet, and roaches are attracted to it as much as they are to grease. But of course, when they get to it and dive in to have a sip, they'll discover they can't swim. This realization is followed by their slow demise. Kind of morbid, I know, but at least they won't be walking all over your furniture.

GET COFFEE STAINS OUT OF YOUR CARPET

DILEMMA:

You had a bunch of friends over for afternoon coffee, but one of them showed up drunk and belligerent and spilled her cup of joe all over your Turkish carpet.

SOLUTION:

The water you boiled spinach with and an old toothbrush will make the coffee stains come off the carpet. Dab the toothbrush in the spinach water, scrub, and use a towel to absorb it. A few repetitions immediately after the spill should do the job.

WHY THIS WORKS:

Coffee stains are hard to remove with soap because they contain acids such as tannins and polyphenols. Spinach contains a substance called oxalic acid, which can have a bleaching effect on acidic coffee stains.

WARNING: Spinach water also contains chlorophyll, so don't try this on a white carpet—it could leave green stains.

DILEMMA:

To perfect the mood for your housewarming party, you lit tea candles and placed them on the floor all across the room. It was pretty, but also very messy. Now the floor and your guests' shoes have been smeared with candle wax.

SOLUTION:

You can probably pick a bunch of it off the floor and the shoes with your fingers, but persistently clingy wax can be removed with paper towels and an iron. Heat the iron, place a paper towel on top of the problem area, and iron over the towel evenly.

WHY THIS WORKS:

The paper towel's complex fiber structure, full of air pockets, makes it highly absorbent and optimal for this task. When heat is applied from one side of the paper towel, the candle wax melts again and clings to the other side.

-HOW TO-
CLEAN YOUR TOILET BOWL

DILEMMA:

It's the house chore you dread the most—cleaning the toilet bowl. It disgusts you just thinking about what that funky brown ring consists of, but you know it has to go.

SOLUTION:

Pour a small cupful of mouthwash in the toilet bowl. After fifteen to twenty minutes, dip a toilet brush in the water and give all surfaces a quick wipe. Just one flush and you're done.

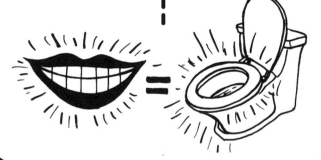

WHY THIS WORKS:

Mouthwash disinfects your oral cavity and gives your teeth a little shine. When you give your toilet bowl the same rinse treatment, the ceramic will be as shiny as your molars.

DILEMMA:

You always use your fingers to wipe clear a section of the vanity mirror to admire your postshower self. But isn't there a better way?

SOLUTION:

Slice a potato in half and rub the inner surface against the glass.

WHY THIS WORKS:

The juice of a potato is full of proteins and starch granules, which help absorb moisture. Also, the lecithin in the potatoes—the stuff that emulsifies, or disperses, liquid—repels water and makes it harder for it to remain on the glass.

PREVENT SOAP FROM BECOMING RUNNY

DILEMMA:

You love using bar soap in the shower, but you settle for liquid soap because the bars always become runny and messy, leaving residue all over the place.

SOLUTION:

Stick a strip of aluminum foil on the bottom of the bar of soap to prevent the runny scum from getting all over your sink and tub.

WHY THIS WORKS:

The aluminum foil reduces the surface area of the soap, which in turn reduces its susceptibility to runniness. If you don't have aluminum foil, use plastic wrap or a piece of cardboard.

MAKE A TINY PIECE OF SOAP BIG AGAIN

DILEMMA:

With all the scrubbing and foaming going on, a standard bar of soap usually shrinks to a slippery little dime-size clump in just a week. How can you sustain your soap dependency without running to the drugstore all the time for new supplies?

SOLUTION:

Stick the dying soap in the microwave and watch it grow back into a usable size.

WHY THIS WORKS:

In its normally marketed form, bar soap is hard but contains air and water. A few things happen when the soap nub is heated up in the microwave: The soap softens; the water inside vaporizes and forms bubbles, and the air inside expands. These expansions create pressure pockets, stretching the softened soap and making it bigger. When the microwave stops, so does the bubbling and expanding. The finished product might look a little lumpy, but in terms of usability, it's just as effective as it was in its original form.

-HOW TO-
MAKE A FRAYED TOOTHBRUSH LOOK NEW AGAIN

DILEMMA:

Your mom always tells you to replace your toothbrush when the bristles start fraying, but the way you brush your teeth, that would be way too often for it to be worth your money. Isn't there a way to make a toothbrush last longer?

SOLUTION:

Next time your toothbrush starts looking more like a garden rake, put it under hot water for a few minutes and stretch the softened bristles back out straight.

WHY THIS WORKS:

The bristles of a toothbrush are made of thermoplastic, which becomes softer in hotter temperatures. When you soak them in hot water, they become temporarily more flexible and you can shape them the way you want. Once the brush head cools down again, it's as good as new.

CLEAN A WINDOW WITHOUT LEAVING STREAKS

DILEMMA:

Windows get dirty from wind, rain, pigeon poop, dog paws, people pressing their noses and fingers against them, and other sources of grime. But cleaning them with squeegees and glass cleaner is drippy and messy and always leaves skid marks on the panes.

SOLUTION:

Dampen a sheet of newspaper with some water or glass cleaner and use that to wipe your windows clean.

WHY THIS WORKS:

Newsprint—the stuff newspapers are made of—has a highly absorbent substance in it called lignin. Lignin's usually removed from other types of paper because it causes yellowing and brittleness, but because newspapers are meant to be low cost, not high maintenance, they still have this naturally absorptive stuff—and they're great as quick, disposable squeegee alternatives.

-HOW TO-
GET PERMANENT PEN MARKS OFF YOUR WINDOW

DILEMMA:

Your kid just learned how to write in cursive, and now he's written his name all over his bedroom window with a permanent marker.

SOLUTION:

Scrub over your kid's genius graffiti with chalk to make those seemingly permanent marks disappear.

WHY THIS WORKS:

Chalk is made of calcium carbonate, the same stuff used in toothpaste to remove plaque from your teeth. It has a grainy texture and pointed edges, which sand the permanent-marker marks down just enough to get them off the glass.

DILEMMA:

You got a new puppy, and now your once beautifully green lawn has bare brown patches all over it from dog pee.

SOLUTION:

Pour some beer on the problem areas, making sure the foam's covering all the naked spots. The grass will be greener in no time.

WHY THIS WORKS:

Beer has fermented sugars in it, which can act as natural fertilizer. The dying grass will feed on these sugars, detrimental fungi will die, and your lawn will start looking normal again.

KEEP PIGEONS AWAY FROM YOUR WINDOWSILL

DILEMMA:

The pigeons outside your window are getting out of hand. They congregate on your sill, poop on your plants, and invite their friends. Isn't there a harmless way to ban them from your windowsill once and for all?

SOLUTION:

Tape sharpened pencils around the periphery of the plant pots or boxes to deter the pigeons from wanting to land there.

WHY THIS WORKS:

Pigeons always check before they land, and spikes don't look very inviting to them. The vanguard searching for a perching spot won't choose your windowsill or balcony, and once they start congregating elsewhere, that's where their friends will join them. Larger professional buildings often use short metal spikes to prevent pigeons from landing on their façades or on statues.

DILEMMA:

You're going out of town for a week and taking your two kids, your dog, and your cat with you. But who's going to water the basil plant?

SOLUTION:

Your baby's disposable diapers are useful for more than just absorbing poop and pee. Soak one of the butt-huggers in a tray of water and place the plant pot on top of it to create your own auto-watering device.

WHY THIS WORKS:

The cushy part of the diaper is made of cotton and absorbent polymer powder, which is what keeps baby bums dry. This synthetic, hydrophilic material can store plenty of liquid and allows the soil to slowly absorb the water through the drain holes of the pot as needed, making it the perfect substitute for hiring a plant caretaker or letting the plant wilt and die.

REVIVE A DYING PLANT

DILEMMA:

Your basil plant's not looking so hot these days. You've been giving it a lot of water, but weeks of clouds and no sun have rendered it mildewy and sick-looking.

SOLUTION:

Plants like to eat garlic, too. Next time you water your plant, grate one clove of garlic and mix it into about two cups of water, then use this garlic water to soak the roots. Your plant should revive itself in no time.

WHY THIS WORKS:

Garlic has an antifungal compound called phytoncide, which can kill fungus on roots and help control and prevent the spread of disease.

DILEMMA:

Your boyfriend finally gave you flowers for Valentine's Day after five years of nothing, and you want them to last as long as possible without drying up and wilting.

SOLUTION:

A few drops of bleach work as well as that plant fertilizer they give you at the flower shop. If you don't have bleach, copper can do the deed: just drop a penny in the water instead.

WHY THIS WORKS:

Chlorine bleach, the kind you use at home, has disinfecting properties that prevent bacteria growth and keep plant stems from becoming mildewy, allowing flowers to stay healthy and pretty for longer. Prefer to use a penny? Copper is also a natural fungicide and can prevent bacterial growth on the stems, thus prolonging plant life.

MAKE TARNISHED SILVER JEWELRY SHINY AGAIN

DILEMMA:

Your great-aunt from hell is visiting next weekend, and you know she'll want to see you sporting that ugly silver bracelet she gave you for your high school graduation years ago. The problem is, it's turned dirty and black from neglect.

SOLUTION:

Boil a pot of water with a sheet of aluminum foil in it. Sprinkle baking soda and salt in the water and place your bracelet on the aluminum foil so that they're touching. After a few minutes, you'll see that the jewelry is not black but a shiny silver again.

WHY THIS WORKS:

Silver tarnishes when sulfur attaches to it, forming a black silver-sulfide coating on the surface. But when you put baking soda, salt, and aluminum together, a small electrolytic current is produced and pulls the sulfur atoms right off.

DILEMMA:

You want to wear your old friendship necklace to your ten-year high school reunion, but it's caught in a very complicated tangle with the rest of your long-unworn accessories. It could be another ten years before you actually get the thing out of its mess and put it on.

SOLUTION:

Sprinkle some baby powder at the nucleus of the tangle and watch your necklace—and your temper—ease out of its tension-filled mess.

WHY THIS WORKS:

Baby powder is usually made of ground talc or cornstarch, both of which are supersoft and fine and can fit in almost any crevice. It acts as a lubricant that reduces the friction causing the knots, softening kinks and loosening tangles.

MAKE A HOMEMADE SCRATCHING POLE FOR YOUR CAT

DILEMMA:

Your cat loves to sharpen his claws on your furniture. Even if you buy him a scratching pole, he still opts for the legs of your expensive wooden dinner table. You've already had the legs replaced twice, so it's time to think of a way to cat-proof the thing.

SOLUTION:

Wrap lengths of rope tightly around the table legs, and tie them at the top and bottom so they don't loosen and fall off.

WHY THIS WORKS:

Cats like to scratch at anything that has a satisfying texture. Rope, stringy and rough, can be easily molded into any shape, including that of table legs. You can also use corrugated cardboard, which is not as malleable but is equally satisfying to your kitty.

DILEMMA:

You're pulling an all-nighter to cram for a test, and you need a quick break—some easy entertainment—but all you have are those giant headphones you use to drown out street noise.

SOLUTION:

Plug your headphones into the microphone jack of your computer and use a music-playing program to receive and amplify your beautiful voice, instantly turning the headphones into a karaoke mic.

WHY THIS WORKS:

Headphones and microphones work pretty much the same way, except the process of translating electric currents to sound is reversed. The main components in headphones are a little magnet and a coil of wire. When you run an electric current through the wire, it moves the electrical parts to produce sound. When the current is reversed, it goes backward from the mic jack to the computer and produces a current that represents your voice.

CHAPTER FIVE:
BEHIND THE CUPBOARD DOOR

In Japan, cooking spaces are often small and cramped. Some kitchens consist of nothing more than a single burner and a minifridge near the entrance of the apartment. But this hasn't stopped the Japanese from concocting delicious home-cooked meals—often, it just brings an extra level of creative invention to the cutting board. The Japanese kitchen is especially fertile ground for developing urawaza, with hundreds of cooking shortcuts and cleaning tricks that make you wonder why you bought all those products and gadgets overflowing from your cabinets and onto your counter space.

DILEMMA:
You're making cookies tomorrow for a company party, but your box of sugar is all clumped up and impossible to measure.

SOLUTION:
Put a small piece of bread in the sugar for at least six hours. When you come back to it, the sugar will be as fine and grainy as a white-sand beach in Hawaii.

WHY THIS WORKS:

Sugar clumps together because the surface dries out and hardens after a long time on the shelf and the particles start to stick to each other. When you put something moist, like bread, in with the sugar, the foreign object lends some of its moisture to the glued-together surface, allowing it to soften and letting the crystals fall apart. If you don't have bread, use a piece of peeled fruit or even a dampened paper towel.

MAKE EGG SALAD WITHOUT CHOPPING

DILEMMA:

Your kids love to eat egg-salad sandwiches for lunch, but chopping up all those eggs is a big pain in the butt.

SOLUTION:

Next time you buy a bag of oranges at the supermarket, make sure you hold on to the mesh bag they come in. Squeezing hard-boiled eggs through one of these sacks will give you finely chopped egg bits—completely knife-free.

WHY THIS WORKS:

Woven polypropylene mesh bags, durable and airy, also happen to have perfectly spaced gaps for mashing eggs.

DILEMMA:

You cook everything under the sun in your favorite aluminum pot, and now it's turning black and crusty inside.

SOLUTION:

Cut a couple thin slices from an apple and put them in the pot with just enough water to cover the grime. Bring the apple water to a boil and let it simmer for ten minutes. When that's done, wipe the stains off clean with soap and a sponge.

WHY THIS WORKS:

Apples contain malic acid, which contributes to the tart flavor of the fruit but is also a really good substance for removing crud from the bottom of a cooking pot. Malic acid works best on aluminum pots and less effectively on stainless steel.

-HOW TO-
CLEAN UP SPILLED EGG YOLK

DILEMMA:

The egg was supposed to crack into the pan—not on the floor. Now there's gook all over the linoleum.

SOLUTION:

Sprinkle some table salt on the spilled egg and wait ten minutes for it to soak in, then sweep the egg yolk right off the floor with a broom.

WHY THIS WORKS:

The salt dissolves the lipoproteins in egg yolk, which changes its texture from gooey to nongooey, making it easier to clean.

DILEMMA:

You bought a pair of mangoes at the supermarket, but the first one you opened tastes more like a lemon.

SOLUTION:

Draw a bath—not for yourself, for your mangoes! Let the mangoes relax in a tub of hot tap water for ten minutes (not too much longer, because they'll become shriveled like prunes), and that sweetness you crave will be yours in no time at all.

WHY THIS WORKS:

Unlike some other fruits, mangoes continue to ripen even after they're picked. When you put them in hot water, you speed up the starch-to-sugar conversion process, which usually takes a few days.

WARNING: Make sure the water's not hotter than 110 degrees—the heat could damage your mangoes permanently.

-HOW TO-
PEEL A BOILED EGG EFFORTLESSLY

DILEMMA:
Your favorite breakfast? Hard-boiled eggs on toast. The only thing you hate about it is the laborious process of peeling the shells.

SOLUTION:
Pour some water in a hard plastic container and put the boiled eggs inside. Close the lid, then shake the container up and down for about ten seconds. When you open the lid, your eggs will have cracks in them. Just pull off the top piece of each shell, and you'll find that they're much easier to peel.

WHY THIS WORKS:

When eggs are heated up in their shells, the thin skin layer sticks to the egg whites, making them difficult to peel. When you shake the container up and down, the shell cracks and the skin rips, and air and water get between the skins and the egg whites, separating them and making them much easier to peel.

-HOW TO-
GET RID OF TUPPERWARE STINK

DILEMMA:

That Japanese curry you made for the potluck was a big hit, but now the Tupperware you took it in smells like chicken and spices.

SOLUTION:

Chop a handful of cabbage into chunks and put them inside the Tupperware. Close the lid and leave it as is for about half a day. When you come back to it later, the smell will be gone.

WHY THIS WORKS:

Chopped cabbage has an enormous amount of surface area, which is effective in absorbing smells from the air around it. Cabbage also has active enzymes and sulfur compounds that can destroy substances that leave residual smells.

GET RID OF TEA STAINS ON YOUR MUG

DILEMMA:

You drink a lot of tea at home, but sometimes you forget to do the dishes right away. Now you have a cabinet full of tea-stained mugs.

SOLUTION:

Peel an orange or a lemon, and sprinkle some salt on the inside of the peel, then rub the peel against the tea stains on your mug.

WHY THIS WORKS:

The natural oils and acidity of the peel make it an ideal stain remover, and salt acts as an abrasive to scrub the persistent stains.

DILEMMA:

Your morning routine: Wake up, buy coffee, rush to work, put coffee down at desk, run to morning meeting, forget coffee, come back. The coffee's cold and bitter by the time you have time to drink it—and you will be, too, if you don't come up with a quick solution.

SOLUTION:

Add a few grains of salt to your cold cup and nuke it in the microwave for a minute. You'll notice that your coffee tastes almost as good as when it was freshly brewed.

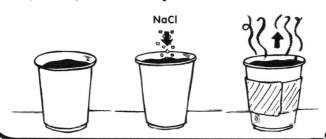

NaCl

WHY THIS WORKS:

When coffee becomes stale, it loses its aromatic aura and the bitterness kicks in. Salt naturally reduces bitterness, allowing the lovely bean flavor to prevail again.

-HOW TO-
QUICKLY CHILL A CHAMPAGNE BOTTLE

DILEMMA:

It happens to everyone—you forget your wedding anniversary or some other important cause for celebration, and your wife's headed home from work, like, right now. You dig up that old champagne bottle from the pantry, but you don't want her to think you forgot to chill it. It's bad enough you don't have a present, or even a cheesy card.

SOLUTION:

Place the bottle in an ice bucket, but instead of just throwing ice in with it, alternate layers of ice with layers of sprinkled salt, which will help chill the champagne much faster than if you just use ice.

WHY THIS WORKS:

As the ice melts, the salt dissolves in the water. Because the salt-water solution and the ice are only in equilibrium at a temperature below freezing, more of the ice melts almost immediately. This process is called latent heat of fusion: Salt makes ice melt faster, and the whole system of cooling becomes more intense.

DILEMMA:

Your kid wants to drink beer real bad. Of course you said no—he's only six—but you relented when he asked you if he could at least pour it into your glass. The problem is, your beer mug is now 80 percent foam.

SOLUTION:

Sprinkle several drops of olive oil into your sea of foam and watch the bubbles subside.

WHY THIS WORKS:

Though all beers have a certain amount of intentional foam created by carbon dioxide, a brash pouring job can cause excess air bubbles to form in the liquid. Oil molecules have hydrophobic ends that attach to the bubble-stabilizing proteins in the foam and pull them out, reducing the foam. If you don't have olive oil handy, lightly touch your finger to the foam surface—the oils from your skin have the same effect.

GET BURN MARKS OFF THE OUTSIDE OF A PAN

DILEMMA:
You've made your scrambled-eggs-and-bacon breakfast, but even after you soap the pan with a sponge and rinse it, some stubborn burn and oil marks remain on the outer rim.

SOLUTION:
Crumble an eggshell, then rub the fragments against the problem areas for a clean, shiny finish.

WHY THIS WORKS:

The calcium carbonate in eggshells gives them an abrasive texture, which makes them work like a loofah. Also, small amounts of egg-white residue on the inner surface of the shells can help pick up loose particles and give the pan a polished finish.

-HOW TO-

KEEP A SODA BOTTLE FIZZY LONGER

DILEMMA:

Those two-liter bottles of soda are great for saving money. The problem is, you live alone, and you rarely finish the entire bottle before it becomes flat.

SOLUTION:

After every pour, squeeze the sides of the bottle so that the plastic crunches inward. Do this before you twist the cap back on for a significantly longer soda life span.

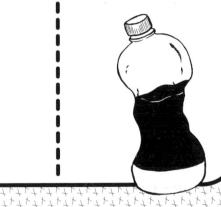

WHY THIS WORKS:

Carbonation is caused when carbon dioxide is dissolved in water to make carbonic acid. When you open the bottle, the solution is depressurized, and the gases start escaping, producing satisfying bubbles. Squeezing out the residual air from the bottle and capping it will slow down the escaping process—called effervescence—and leave you with a better chance of having fizzy soda when you come back to it later.

PREVENT BOILING PASTA FROM SPILLING OVER IN A POT

DILEMMA:

Making pasta is supposed to be simple and worry-free, but it's almost guaranteed that the water will spill over if you leave it on the stove unmonitored. Nine times out of ten, you end up spending more time cleaning the stovetop than eating your dinner.

SOLUTION:

Put a conventional ashtray inside the water upside down and you'll never have to worry about overenthusiastic bubbles spilling over again. Just don't use a dirty one! That would be gross.

WHY THIS WORKS:

Spillovers are caused by bubbles that have a hard time popping. Usually, bubbles pop by the time they reach the surface, but the starch from the pasta makes the bubbles more durable. These long-lasting, pop-resistant bubbles rise to the surface, stack up above each other, and cause the water they displace to spill over. But when you put the ashtray inside the pot, the bubbles that form inside the dome of the ashtray combine to make a giant bubble that escapes through the cigarette-holder gaps before it has a chance to make the water splash.

DILEMMA:

You had a basketful of garlic bread and a mountain of pesto pasta for dinner, and now you can't get rid of that awful garlic breath. How are you going to kiss your first date good-bye at the end of the night smelling like this?

SOLUTION:

Drink a cup of green tea shortly after a garlicky meal and you can still have a refreshing after-dinner kiss.

WHY THIS WORKS:

Green-tea particles attract and shrink odorous bacteria, and the catechin prevents their proliferation and keeps the inside of your mouth stink-free.

CHAPTER SIX:
LAUNDRY SHORTCUTS

Despite space constraints and energy concerns, most Japanese households—even studio apartments for the young, single urban dweller—have washing machines, either outside on the tiny balcony or in a nook by the bathroom. A lot of people still hang-dry their wash with little plastic clothespins that string down from a circular hanger or on a cord strung across the room. The Japanese are also much more particular about following washing instructions and hand-washing woolens and lingerie. But despite the attention given to garment care, there's always the occasional problem that leaves you stumped—a pair of socks that continue to smell like sweaty feet after multiple washes, stains that just don't come out, the sweater that shrinks, the shirt that stinks. These urawaza are useful all around for everyone who does laundry—or needs to.

DILEMMA:

After wearing the same generic white T-shirt day in and day out for a year, you're starting to notice growing smudges of yellow right where your armpits touch the fabric.

SOLUTION:

Don't let your new T-shirt meet the same fate. Before you wear it out, spritz some adhesive spray on the inside of the armpit and iron the area from the outside. Your pits will stay free of yellow stains.

WHY THIS WORKS:

Dirt and grime that gets between a shirt's threads washes off fairly easily in the laundry. But underarm stains on your shirts appear when they get *into* your threads—these are the stains that are impossible to get out and eventually show up as permanent ugly yellow patches. The glue will seal up the tiny capillaries in the threads, preventing anything else from getting inside. Think Scotchgard, but a more informal version.

GET RED WINE STAINS OUT OF YOUR WHITES

DILEMMA:

Cabernet Sauvignon is the partygoer's greatest nemesis. They almost shouldn't serve it at weddings, period, because when the crowd goes wild and the bride goes crazy, it almost always sprinkles the bride's gown with ruby-red dots.

SOLUTION:

Mix hydrogen peroxide with liquid soap to create a great natural red wine remover.

WHY THIS WORKS:

Peroxide is an oxidizer, bleaching the color compounds and pigments in the wine. Pigments are hard to get out because they're not water soluble, but soap molecules—which have a hydrophobic end and a hydrophilic end—grab onto the pigment compound and allow the peroxide to react with the pigments that cause the stain.

DILEMMA:

You just bought a motorcycle and a cool new black leather jacket to go with it. But there's one problem: The jacket won't stay clean. And after taking out a loan to buy the two-wheeler, it's not like you can afford professional leather cleaning every time you go out on the town.

SOLUTION:

Make it a habit to give your jacket a quick cleaning every time you eat a banana. Leave the banana peel out to dry overnight. When ready, rub the inside of the peel against the surface of the leather. Follow up by buffing the jacket with the outside surface of the peel for a finishing polish.

WHY THIS WORKS:

The average banana peel contains 30 to 40 percent tannin, the stuff used in commercial leather cleaners. When dried, the peel makes a natural leather cleaner, and the outside of the banana peel contains wax, giving leather a perfect top coat.

KEEP YOUR SHIRT CLEAN

DILEMMA:

You're not a sweaty guy, but the sleeve ends and collar of your shirt inevitably get soiled from daily use. You need to figure out a way to keep them clean without taking them to the dry cleaners every day.

SOLUTION:

The key is to keep these problem points well protected. Sprinkle them lightly with baby powder before you go out, and you can prevent unwarranted soiling—and save on your dry-cleaning bill.

WHY THIS WORKS:

The baby powder keeps oil and grime from your neck and the outdoor world off the cuffs without damaging the fabric of your shirt. (This works best on white or light-colored shirts.)

-HOW TO-
GET RID OF CIGARETTE STENCH

DILEMMA:
Going out to nightclubs is fun, but your clothes always smell like crap the next day from other people's sweat, spilled alcohol, and—worst of all—stale cigarette smoke.

SOLUTION:
Moisten a towel and place it on a flat surface over your stinky shirt, then iron the towel with the shirt beneath it. The towel will soak up the odor, making your shirt smell fresh again.

WHY THIS WORKS:

The steam from the iron dissolves the tar from the cigarettes and removes the smelly molecules from your shirt.

-HOW TO-
MAKE DIRT-STAINED SOCKS WHITE AGAIN

DILEMMA:

White socks don't stay white for very long. They accumulate sweat, and you're always walking on dirty surfaces without knowing it. Just dumping them in the washer doesn't get rid of the grimy stains on the soles of your feet anymore.

SOLUTION:

Grab some of those glass marbles from the bottom of the fish tank and put a handful in each sock. Tie the socks with rubber bands so the marbles don't fall out and stick them in the laundry with the rest of your stuff.

WHY THIS WORKS:

The marbles work as extra agitators, moving water in and around the socks more quickly and working as though you're hyper-scrubbing them. The water surges extra-fast, the soap bubbles become ultrafine, and your socks become superclean.

WARNING: Front-load, high-efficiency washers that leverage the impact of falling clothes can shatter the marbles.

-HOW TO-

GET RID OF PERSISTENT SOCK SMELL

DILEMMA:
No matter how many times you wash them, your socks still smell like feet and fungus.

SOLUTION:
After your next laundry day, soak those stinky socks in a vodka-water solution for a little while.

WHY THIS WORKS:

Your socks stink because certain bacteria remain on them even after they're washed with detergent. Vodka, basically just a combination of ethanol and water, has a high enough alcohol content to have disinfecting and odor-removing characteristics. Or, if you don't want to waste your liquor-cabinet stash on your feet, use vinegar, a fermented version of ethanol with acetic and citric acids that help with cleaning.

KEEP SHOES DRY AND FRESH

DILEMMA:

Smelly, musty shoes are the worst. But the inevitable stink plagues all great kicks when they're worn day in and day out. How do you keep your shoe closet from smelling like one giant dirty foot?

SOLUTION:

Newspapers are great moisture absorbers and odor removers. Just roll up a couple sheets at a time and place them between and inside your shoes.

WHY THIS WORKS:

Newsprint—uncoated, cheap paper with a lot of surface area—acts like an activated carbon filter, picking up any moisture it comes in contact with. When you crumple it inside shoes, it picks up all the moisture in them. The musty smell is a side effect of mold, which can grow only in the presence of excess water, so the absorptive properties of the newspaper kill two birds with one stone.

DILEMMA:

You want to sport some creative permanent-marker art on your plain white T-shirts, but it's impossible to prevent crinkles and smudges in the process.

SOLUTION:

Soak the shirt's surface with hairspray and draw on it as easily as you write on paper with a pencil.

WHY THIS WORKS:

The copolymer in the hairspray prevents smearing by blocking the oils in the permanent marker from getting between the fibers. The spray also hardens the surface, preventing crinkles.

RESTORE A SHRUNKEN SWEATER TO ITS ORIGINAL SIZE

DILEMMA:

Oops! You put your favorite wool sweater in the washing machine and dryer along with your socks, and now it would barely fit your ten-year-old niece.

SOLUTION:

Immerse the sweater in a water-plus-hair-conditioner solution for half an hour, and your sweater will magically expand to its original size.

WHY THIS WORKS:

Woolen apparel shrinks because water gets between the fibers and causes them to tangle. There's a substance in most hair conditioners called amodimethicone that untangles these fibers—just like it does to your hair.

DILEMMA:

You knit your little dog a sweater using fancy techniques to create an argyle print, only to realize it's way too big and lumpy.

SOLUTION:

Immerse the sweater in lukewarm soapy water. Squeeze the suds through it a couple times, then squeegee the water out by wrapping it up in a towel like a sushi roll. Then lay it out flat and reshape it with your fingers.

WHY THIS WORKS:

When you squeeze the sudsy sweater fibers together, you're making them intermingle and then deliberately "blocking" them while they're tangled—kind of like weaving blades of grass together and reshaping them into a basket.

MAKE YOUR TROUSERS STAY ON A HANGER

DILEMMA:

You store your work pants on cheap plastic hangers, but they keep slipping off every time you're browsing your wardrobe.

SOLUTION:

It's all about placement. Instead of folding the entire garment over the hanger, cross one pant leg over the other.

WHY THIS WORKS:

Trousers and other things fall off your hangers because of two factors—imbalance and slipperiness. When you cross one pant leg over the other, you are solving the imbalance problem with evenness on both sides. Also, the friction between the two pant legs prevents slipperiness, allowing your pants to stay put and hanging.

DILEMMA:

You have some highly confidential documents (yeah, OK, secret love letters) you don't want anyone to read. You don't even want to take them to the office to shred—what if they fall out of your bag and someone finds out you're stalking your intern?

SOLUTION:

Put the incriminating papers inside a stocking, tie the stocking up, and throw it in the washing machine.

WHY THIS WORKS:

By the time your secrets have gone through a full wash cycle in the stocking, the paper will be shredded to bits and the ink—depending on what kind you used—will be more or less smudgy and illegible. And nobody will even think to pick that stuff out of the garbage!

CHAPTER SEVEN:
STREET SMARTS FOR
THE GREAT OUTDOORS

Most of the time, going out in Tokyo is fun. And then there's the rainy season. For about a month and a half, usually starting in early June, it rains pretty much nonstop, and the city is covered in clouds and umbrellas. Rainy season is usually followed by a very humid, mosquito-infested summer.

But even when it pours, you still have to brave the weather and go to work. And when the street festivals and fireworks displays start up in the post–rainy season months, it's definitely worth trekking outdoors, despite the mugginess, to enjoy them.

Few people commute by car in Japan—most cities have hyperefficient, inexpensive public transportation systems—so you need to learn how to keep your cool no matter what the external conditions, whether you're making your way to work on a public bus on a hot summer day or renting a car to go skiing up in the mountains on a cold winter night.

DILEMMA:

The rain outside is borderline torrential, but all you have is a crappy old water-resistant military jacket you inherited from your great-grandpa. Instead of keeping you warm and dry, this old thing soaks up water like a sponge, and by the time you get to where you need to be, you're feeling damp and musty, and the jacket's dripping like a golden retriever that just went swimming in a lake.

SOLUTION:

Even an old jacket can learn new tricks. When you come home from a rainy day out, evenly blow-dry your moist jacket's outer surface to make it waterproof again.

WHY THIS WORKS:

A lot of outdoorsy jackets are made waterproof with a durable water-repellent (DWR) coating. Over time, the coating starts to deteriorate, and it gradually flattens out completely to the point where it's not working. Applying high heat realigns the molecules of the fluorochemicals in the DWR coating and activates the water-repelling properties. If you don't have the patience to blow-dry your jacket, consider putting it in a clothes dryer on high heat for half an hour.

SOOTHE ITCHY MOSQUITO BITES

DILEMMA:

Every time you take out the trash, you come back with half a dozen unbearably itchy bite marks. Calamine lotion and hydrocortisone do nothing to relieve the constant tickle.

SOLUTION:

It's easy to alleviate mosquito-bite itch without dousing yourself with anti-itch cream: Either slap a piece of adhesive tape onto the area of the bite, or use a drinking straw to suck the discomfort away.

WHY THIS WORKS:

There's no major science behind these strategies—unless you call distraction a science. Mosquito-bite itch is caused by the bug's saliva, which makes little tension-filled round dots swell on your skin. The adhesive tape applies pressure to the whole area, so you don't want to scratch; sucking with a straw creates just enough countertension to alleviate the itch.

DILEMMA:

You're having a barbecue in the woods, and you have all your bases covered—almost. Who knew hordes of mosquitoes would swarm around the hot dogs?

SOLUTION:

Add a few drops of lavender oil to a glass of water and wipe down the table, the chairs, and the barbecue pit with the mixture—and wipe some on your exposed skin while you're at it.

WHY THIS WORKS:

Lavender oil smells like peace and relaxation to humans, but to mosquitoes, it reeks like dog poo. Okay, maybe not dog poo. But it repels them enough so that they won't suck your blood when your furniture—and your skin—is doused with it.

-HOW TO-
GET RID OF POISON OAK AND POISON IVY ITCH

DILEMMA:

You thought it would be romantic to take your date hiking off the beaten path. It didn't occur to you that your path was unbeaten because of the abundant poison ivy bushes beyond the "Do Not Enter" sign until you were red and itchy all over.

SOLUTION:

Spray or slather old-fashioned white shoe polish on the problem areas and you'll feel its soothing effect in no time. Plus, you'll be shiny and white like a pair of new kicks.

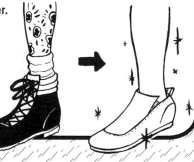

WHY THIS WORKS:

Traditionally, shoe polish contains pipe clay, which is similar to calamine lotion in its ability to soothe itchiness.

DILEMMA:
The roads are slippery with winter slush and rain, but you still want to wear your Prada pumps to work.

SOLUTION:
Apply two Band-Aids to the sole of each shoe—one on the ball and one on the heel—and your fancy kicks will be as water-resistant as those yellow rubber boots you wore as a kid.

WHY THIS WORKS:

Rainy-day slipperiness happens when water gets between the soles of your shoes and the ground's surface. The gauze patches at the center of a bandage absorb water and greatly improve traction.

-HOW TO-
PREVENT YOUR GLASSES FROM FOGGING UP

DILEMMA:

You look fly in your new titanium glasses, but the problem isn't how you look. It's how you see. The lenses fog up every time you cook pasta, walk in the rain, or lounge in a hot tub with a pretty girl.

SOLUTION:

Crack a raw egg open and dip your fingers into the egg white. Smear a thin film evenly across both sides of each lens and head into the kitchen—or the hot tub—for fog-free 20/20 vision!

WHY THIS WORKS:

The main ingredient in egg white is protein, which is highly soluble in water, and a layer of protein coating the lens surface allows it to repel steam.

DILEMMA:

Your new car has all-wheel drive, winter tires, a V-8 engine, and a ski rack. It's perfect for going up to the mountains on winter weekends, except the damn doors keep freezing shut overnight.

SOLUTION:

Before you head up to the winter wonderland, spray the rubber gaskets between the doors and the car body with nonstick cooking spray. This is most effective when applied to a dry surface, so remember to do it before you plunge into the snowstorm.

WHY THIS WORKS:

Nonstick cooking spray is oily, and the thin film lubricates the surfaces, preventing water from collecting on the rubber and the metal and freezing them together. It's kind of like coating the surface of a pan with oil—once you do that, when you sprinkle the pan with droplets of water, they'll just bead up.

-HOW TO-
BOOST A CAR BATTERY

DILEMMA:

Uh oh! You left your headlights on while you slept over at your boyfriend's house, and now the car won't start. All you have right now is a hangover, a bottle of aspirin, and a screwdriver (the tool, not the drink), and you just want to get home and sleep without having to call a tow truck.

SOLUTION:

Open the battery cell covers with a screwdriver and drop two tablets of aspirin in each cell. Wait a few minutes, then start the car.

WHY THIS WORKS:

The acetylsalicylic acid in the aspirin combines with the sulfuric acid in the battery, stimulates the electrolytes, and provides one good boost to the fading battery.

WARNING: The aspirin is great for a boost but bad for the life span of the battery, so don't do it too often. Also, be careful when you open the covers!

-HOW TO-
CLEAN YOUR WINDSHIELD

DILEMMA:
Wiper fluid is good for clearing up most of the windshield, but it always leaves the edges even dirtier than before.

SOLUTION:
Remove the tape from a cassette—if you still have any around—shape it into a ball, stuff it into the foot of an old stocking, and tie the tip closed. You've just made your very own window wiper that won't leave streaks and stains all over the place.

WHY THIS WORKS:

Most cassette tape is made of ferric oxide and cobalt. In fine powder form, ferric oxide is often used as the finishing polish for jewelry and glasses—in other words, it's great for magnetic storage but also an effective shine enhancer. The stockings are made of nylon, which is sturdy and keeps the tape material in a solid bunch without interfering with its cleaning skills.

FIX A RUSTY BICYCLE

DILEMMA:

You left your mountain bike outside for months, and now it's time to take it for a spin again. The problem is, it's all rusty and squeaky, and you're afraid it'll have trouble shifting gears.

SOLUTION:

Make a paste of three parts salt and one part lemon juice. Apply it to a soft cloth, and use it to rub the rust off the bicycle handles, tire rims, and gears, then rinse it off with water.

WHY THIS WORKS:

Lemon juice contains citric acid, which can dissolve iron oxide, or rust, and the salt works as a gentle abrasive that removes rusty grit.

-HOW TO-
PREVENT FALLING OVER IN A CROWDED BUS

DILEMMA:

Your dreaded morning commute consists of a harrowing forty-five-minute bus ride surrounded by sweaty people who push and shove you when they sway and tumble every time the bus jerks to a stop.

SOLUTION:

Teach this technique to all your fellow passengers: If everyone stands facing the front of the bus with their feet at a forty-five-degree angle, they'll be less likely to fall over everywhere.

WHY THIS WORKS:

This angle is commonly used in professional sports because it's the most balanced, agile resting state. Think of the defensive shuffle on the basketball court, the prematch stance of the sumo wrestler, or the service position at the beginning of a tennis match. Athletes stand like that because no other stance is as sturdy and because it's the easiest position from which to quickly shift to another to adjust to outside factors.

KEEP A CANDLE LIT IN THE WIND

DILEMMA:

A romantic candlelit dinner on the beach? Impossible, you say—the wind would blow the flame out in a second.

SOLUTION:

To make your mood lighting significantly more windproof, wrap the candle tightly with some looseleaf magazine paper, making sure it rises to just above the wick.

WHY THIS WORKS:

In windy weather, even a thicker candle with lots of wax is short-lived because the air will blow out the flame, and even if the flame survives, the wind will cause wax to spill over the sides, shortening the flame's life span. By preventing wind from getting down to where the wick is, however, you not only protect the wick but also prevent the wax from wasting away.

DILEMMA:

You're on an important mission in the treacherous jungles of Malaysia, but you realize you forgot to bring a compass. It's still light out, so you still have a few hours to get to your destination, but how can you tell which direction is south?

SOLUTION:

As long as you have an analog wristwatch, you're going to be OK. Point the hour hand toward the sun and locate the exact midpoint between it and the 12. That midpoint, no matter what time of day it is, will point you south.

WHY THIS WORKS:

In the northern hemisphere, the sun is almost always south of the east-west line, so every time you're pointing toward the sun, you're looking due south. This is accurate up to twenty degrees, depending on the time of day—it's the most accurate at high noon and less so during the early morning or the late afternoon.

GET GUM OUT OF YOUR HAIR

DILEMMA:

You decided to blow giant bubble-gum bubbles in an attempt to entertain your kid cousin. She was entertained, all right—especially when it popped all over your bangs!

SOLUTION:

Rub an ice cube against your gummy hair. After a minute or two, the gum will harden and become easy to remove.

WHY THIS WORKS:

Gum is sticky and stretchy, but cooling it down gets rid of the stretchiness factor, making it breakable instead. Once the gum is broken into little pieces, it doesn't have enough surface area to be sticky anymore.

GET GUM OFF YOUR CLOTHES

DILEMMA:

Sitting down on a park bench is risky: You never know who was there before you, and you never know what kind of gum they were chewing. It could have been that really sticky kind that sticks to your teeth—and your jeans.

SOLUTION:

Pour some tequila on the problem region and let it soak in, then wipe the gum off clean with a paper towel.

WHY THIS WORKS:

The sticky ends of alcohol molecules in the tequila attach to the ends of the gum molecules, pulling them off the fabric and making them seem easier to remove. This works even better if the tequila is chilled, because a cooling effect can then also kick in, making the gum less gooey and more solid.

-HOW TO-

DISCOVER YOUR OWN URAWAZA

Part of the charm of urawaza is that they're all homegrown. Scientists didn't spend hours in a lab pouring coffee on the carpet or rubbing their elbows with avocados—these are solutions and remedies people accidentally discovered while going about their everyday lives. That said, there's always room for more inventive uses of household objects, and you, too, can participate in this phenomenon with some creative experimentation. Here's a step-by-step guide to creating and discovering your own urawaza.

STEP 1:

Consider a lingering dilemma you just haven't been able to figure out how to solve. Maybe you haven't worn your favorite shirt in weeks because of that red wine stain on the left sleeve, or your glasses keep slipping off your face no matter how you adjust them.

STEP 2:

Find potentially useful objects. Look around you. Chances are that there is something in the room that will work to your advantage. Examine the contents of kitchen and bathroom cabinets, desk and dresser drawers, toy chests, your refrigerator, and the garage. Try to look at objects and materials for what they are, what they're made of, and what their nature is rather than what they were originally intended to do.

STEP 3:

Consider the different ways you can use these objects. What are their physical properties? Are they sticky or dry, firm or flexible? Can you disassemble or reshape them, then attach them to or mix them with something else in a potentially useful way? Keep in mind that there are often multiple ways to approach a problem, and that solutions may work to varying degrees. For example, in trying to solve the slippery-eyeglasses problem, try taping a strip of a bandage to the bridge of the nosepiece or a pad to each earpiece, or securing the stems with rubber bands, or putting peanut butter in crevices to prevent them from popping open, or—you get the idea.

STEP 4:

Experiment by putting the promising candidates to work. Use the items under different conditions, and re-create the problem so you can try multiple solutions. To test cleaning a red wine spill, for instance, consider deliberately staining multiple parts of an old rag or shirt and testing each section with a potential solution. Be curious and adventurous, but also be prepared for results that may be less successful than you expected. Some words of wisdom: Don't experiment on something unless you're prepared for a less-than-ideal outcome. Read all warning labels on any products you use or anything you try your urawaza out on, and use common sense. For example, don't pour fabric softener all over a fur coat to see if it will make it softer—try it out first on a tiny corner under the armpit where an unfortunate outcome won't be noticed. Test treatments on separate fabrics or on small, not-readily-visible areas of the clothes you're hoping to use the urawaza on.

STEP 5:

Record your results. Maybe all that trial and error yielded nothing useful. But more often than not, you will have discovered by the end of your experimentation that something came out of it—if only a clear path for what to try next, now that you've discovered fifteen ways not to secure slipping glasses. Be aware that the length of time you soak/boil/rub a certain object can affect the results, so don't be discouraged if a solution you were sure would work didn't fly on an initial test run. Just try it again, but for longer this time.

NAME OF OBJECT	WHERE IT WAS FOUND	WHAT I DID WITH IT

FOR HOW LONG	RESULTS	WARNINGS, HINTS, ETC.

STEP 6:

Share your urawaza. Once you've discovered your little secret, spread the word among friends, family, and the rest of the world. Urawaza are intended to make life better for everyone, and chances are that if your discovery was useful to you, it's probably going to save someone else from a randomly less-than-ideal situation one day.

The thrill of discovering urawaza can be addictive, and advanced practitioners often take the practice a step further in the hunt for the new by reversing the process. Emulate them: Rather than starting with a problem and trying to solve it, begin by contemplating the qualities of everyday materials and extrapolate a problem they might be useful in solving. Then experiment to see if you're right. And, most of all, don't forget to have fun!

Share your own urawaza, and read other new urawaza tips and tricks, at Tokyomango.com.

ACKNOWLEDGMENTS

Many thanks to:
Robert Capps, my editor at *Wired* magazine, who assigned me
a story on urawaza (and sparked my memory and inspiration).

Chronicle Books editors Kevin Toyama and Steve Mockus,
designers Jacob Gardner and Eloise Leigh, managing editor
Doug Ogan, managing editorial assistant Evan Hulka, production coordinators Yolanda Accinelli and Ben Kasman,
copy editor Mark Nichol, and illustrator Joel Holland for making
this book look pretty and professional.

Bob Jacobsen, Harold McGee, Yoji Kobayashi, Yuko Noda, the
Salt Institute, the American Egg Board, the Exploratorium,
Stacy Gebhards, and Cordula Mora for investigating the sci-
ence behind the tricks in this book.

James Lee and Kenji Kushida for their helpful comments on
earlier drafts.

My parents, Sho and Mary Katayama, my brother, Yushi,
and—last but not least—my lovely little dog Ruby, without
whom I never would have survived writing for days on end.